C6
W7
£2

SAD GIRAFFE CAFÉ

Other books by Richard Gwyn

POETRY
Defying Gravity
One Night in Icarus Street
Stone Dog, Flower Red
Walking on Bones
Being in Water
The Pterodactyl's Wing (Ed.)

NOVELS
The Colour of a Dog Running Away
Deep Hanging Out

SAD GIRAFFE CAFÉ

Richard Gwyn

PUBLICATIONS
2010

Published by Arc Publications
Nanholme Mill, Shaw Wood Road
Todmorden OL14 6DA, UK
www.arcpublications.co.uk

Copyright © Richard Gwyn 2010
Design by Tony Ward
Printed in Great Britain by the
MPG Book Group, Bodmin and King's Lynn

978 1906570 45 3 pbk
978 1906570 48 4 hbk

ACKNOWLEDGEMENTS
The author would like to thank the editors of the
following publications in which a number
of these poems have appeared:
Agenda, *Ambit*, *Poetry Wales*, *New Welsh Review* (UK);
Sentence (USA); *Southerly* (Australia).

Cover picture by Alun Hemming

Supported by
ARTS COUNCIL
ENGLAND

Editor for the UK and Ireland: John W Clarke

For Sioned and Rhiannon

CONTENTS

Et puis, et puis encore?
BAUDELAIRE, *Le Voyage*

ACROBATS

The acrobats were packing up the show. They untied the high-wire, collected hoops, poles, buckets, horses, dogs, a lion, two seals, the bearded lady, sand, fire and water. They emptied all of these into one enormous bag, coloured blue, like the sky. The largest acrobat zipped it up. The girl in the tutu and the red-nosed clown massaged it into a rucksack, which the strongman hoisted on his shoulders. They set off, at a quick pace. They could not see me. I had been hiding in an old shoe, behind a rock. I could see the rucksack on the strongman's back. It seemed to shudder and breathe, and made the sound that a thousand starlings make every autumn evening in a certain coastal town in another country.

In the city of Sparta the living was tough. Left out on a hillside as a newborn baby for a night, you soon learned what was what. Then there was fighting to be done, lands to conquer, pillaging and subjugation to carry out. Dignity and an honourable grave. And always those duplicitous Corinthians and superior Athenians to outdo in mortal conflict and in leaving not a hair unscathed. Spears to be polished until they outshone moonbeams, swords to sharpen till the faintest touch would bisect the strongest sinew. If you grew up feeling faint at all this hardship, all this clamouring for blood and death, and longed for just a hint of mystery or tenderness, you were doomed to mockery and insult. I heard them in the schoolyard, the would-be Spartan warriors. Even their swearwords were thoroughbred, while my mouth was full of marbles.

Soldiers came. Administrators followed. They imposed a strict set of rules of conduct. Firstly, the curfew, between the hours of 9 pm and 6 am. Secondly, a restriction on the number of people to be seen together on any one occasion, except in church. Thirdly, that all adults should be fully clothed during hours not covered by the curfew. Fourthly, that the keeping of parrots was strictly forbidden, as were all other birds who mimicked human speech. Fifth, that visits to the doctor were to be confined to those who suffered only curable diseases. Sixth, that all books containing the letter V were to be handed in to the literary authorities. Seventh, that all livestock was to be registered with the appropriate authority, excluding edible fowl and their eggs. Eighth, that black hens were an exception to this last excluding clause and were to be considered property of the Administrators. Ninth, that it was prohibited for dogs to bark between the hours of 9 pm and 6 am, and that if they did so their owners were liable to substantial fines. Tenth, that persons who had dreams containing either (a) elephants; (b) dangerous reptiles, or (c) any variety of crustacean, were to report to the civic authorities at once. Contravention of any of the above stated legislation was to be regarded as a direct challenge to the authority of the Administrators. The rules were posted on a large noticeboard outside the civic hall. On the first night, we were awakened by an explosion. Somebody had fired both barrels of a shotgun into the newly erected noticeboard. All the houses facing the civic hall were searched, but no weapon was found. Four young men were sent to prison.

No one knew where the king was. He had slipped away from the breakfast-room, speaking obscenities. He had not read his newspaper. He had not eaten his two eggs, boiled for precisely four minutes, nor had he finished his hot chocolate. The chancellor was aggrieved: he had, as usual, important issues to bring to the king's attention, issues that could not be postponed. Servants were sent to find the king. They searched the palace and the cellars below the palace. They searched the stables. They looked up trees and peered down wells. The king was not to be found. The queen was reported to be distraught. As the day progressed it became increasingly difficult to keep the news of the king's disappearance within the palace walls. Walls have ears. People talk. In the city, the price of gold began to plummet. But in the evening, the king reappeared, and took his customary place at the head of the dinner table. He was dressed entirely in leaves. Damp soil clung to his face and the royal beard was matted with burrs and spiders' eggs. His hair was crawling with lice and dung-beetles. Everyone was staring at him. *What's the matter with you all?* He growled, reaching for a haunch of meat: *Never felt the need to spend the day beneath the earth?*

15

We have been sold down the river, one of the men wailed, brandishing a leaflet on which were listed the names of all traitors to the king. The river flowed, vast and sedate, through the capital, and its waters lapped the far end of the palace gardens. The king liked to sit in a deck-chair at the river's bank, watching his least favourite ministers being sold down it. Or sailing down it, to be sold. The younger ones went into slavery, suffering many cruelties at the hands of Barbary pirates. Those too old to be of use as forced labourers or rowers of the pirate warships were executed at once to save on rations. Many of the traitors fitted this category. The king sat on his deck-chair and took off his shirt as the barge with this latest band of outcasts passed by. He waved his shirt at the minister for waterways and drains, who was seventy-two years of age and would be of no interest to the pirates. The king liked to take the sun of a morning, was vain enough to believe that a ruddy tan would proclaim him as a hoary son of the soil, and would strengthen his allegiance to the peasantry, who worshipped him.

Because of the many failures encountered in government, the king decided to appoint a new minister for religion. He felt that the country had moved away from God. True, the archbishop was keen to assume a higher profile, but the politicians would not take him seriously, and he suffered badly from halitosis; so they chose a man with a devout manner who professed a profound faith but in fact held no religious convictions whatever. This was an irony of the times, sighed the king, on being informed of the new minister's duplicity and cunning, no better illustrated than by the apparent contradiction contained in the expression 'a confirmed atheist', a phrase which the so-called minister for religious affairs applied to himself when among seditious friends.

Not every one in the country was happy with the news of the king's beheading. There were many for whom the king represented something of supreme value, even if they could not remember exactly what it was. They declared themselves unwilling to live in a republic, which they likened to a state of anarchy. They painted slogans that read: GIVE US BACK OUR KING! This in itself was clearly impossible. But, although the monarchists were in the minority, they were powerful. One day they found a new king and staged a coup. They put the new king on the throne and all the generals who had previously sworn loyalty to the republic now swore loyalty to the king. It was a sunny day in May. There was a public holiday and free cakes. People danced in the streets. Several leading republicans were executed in the prison courtyard. Some months later slogans began appearing on the walls. They said: LONG LIVE THE REPUBLIC! Another impossibility. Another fugitive dream.

Years later, once we had become a Republic again, I was sorting through my wine cellar, when I noticed that the ground's surface had been disturbed. Digging with a trowel, I pulled the king's head from the black soil. The heavy marble showed a face with all the markings of that king's degenerate lineage: bulging eyes, a vacant sneer on his lips – though whether of disdain or congenital cretinism, it was hard to tell – tiny ears, a pointed nose. I carried it upstairs, not knowing quite what I intended, put it on the kitchen table, went to bed. In the morning, the head was not where I had left it: instead the king himself sat at my table, deathly white, covered in bleeding sores. He stared at me as I approached and asked me mournfully for some breakfast. I brought him toast and coffee, which he consumed with evident satisfaction. He told me that he hadn't eaten in years. I too had coffee, and afterwards I smoked. He bummed a cigarette. He always was a parasite. I knew I'd have to get rid of him. Then he told me a secret: I'm going to the races next Saturday, I have a bet on *Lilac Girl*. When he smiled his smile, I began to remember why I had disliked him so intensely. I told him to get out. That Saturday I watched the races on television. *Lilac Girl* came in four lengths clear at thirty-five to one. I was able to buy a lot of very expensive wine.

19

This happened many years ago, when I lived in another country. He was small, slim, muscular. He grew grapes and some vegetables on a plot above the village and he owned a fishing boat, scraping a living from these two sources. He was a quiet man, fleet of foot, sleek of mind. He had been a child during the Italian occupation and picked up odd phrases of that language which he dropped into his speech like splashes of primary colour; the childlike diminutives of the Italian flailing and fluttering ineffectually against the austerity and gravitas of Greek. His knowledge of the world came as a revelation to me, since I had been taught that only educated people could understand the bigger picture. From his boat, he caught octopus, sardines and small fish, *Athirina*, and when I visited the village two years later, he invited Gabriela and me to his table and shared his fish with us, insisting that we eat the heads. Good for the eyes, he said. His own were blue, and narrowed by the habit of staring out to sea. His face was deep, crevassed mahogany. I never saw him wear a pair of shoes, or sandals, even winged ones, though he moved at speed across the thorny paths and clifftops. Perhaps I should have taken account of all this earlier, but there is no going back, not to the places you have left behind.

There they are again, those horses! I was dropping off to sleep this afternoon when one ambled past my patio, head down, exaggerated eye fixed on me. I raised myself onto one elbow in the hammock and watched as it stopped to nibble on some grass, just by the magnolia. I was relaxing back into a more comfortable position when the horse whinnied and then I saw another, plodding up the track from the village, harnessed to a wooden cart. There was a barrel on the cart and a turquoise cockerel perched unsteadily on the horse's back. I recognized the horse, although it came out of a different landscape from the first. It had the same amplified eyes, the same fearful resignation. I would have liked to offer the horses an apple or a carrot, but knew that they would disappear if I approached them. Those horses! They wander around as though they know the place, but with that dismayed uncertainty, and fear of the whip. Small, sturdy, lacking any confidence, and yet being precisely what they are intended to be. I close my eyes and the horses return to some elusive stable in the folds of a moonlit night.

The maize fields are vast and sad in the wind. The tops of the plants bend unwillingly. I know what happens here. It has always remained a secret until now. But for the sake of friendship I will tell you. In July, the castrators will come. They will rip out the genitals of the male plants, so that the females cannot be impregnated and raise bastards. At least, that is what the locals tell the workers. The real story of the maize is more violent still. Groups of young men and women meet after dark, drink absinthe, and fuck beneath the summer moon. In the morning, tired and spent, they retire to the Café D'Artagnan for coffee with milk and croissants. They are recruited by farmers, who drive them to the maize fields. There they begin the tedious task of *le castrage*. The young men begin to feel uncomfortable with this de-seeding of the male plants. Their discomfort translates into physical symptoms: aching sides, persistent headaches and vomiting. Later they will complain of spontaneous ejaculation, green sperm, and will participate in outbreaks of frenzied violence towards other males. In early spring the babies are born: little maize-people, with an obsolete immune system inherited from Aztec forebears. The babies all die before July, when the castration begins again.

RESTLESS GEOGRAPHY

I set out on a journey, but the geography would not stay still, and I ended up somewhere I hadn't intended going.

Do we ever forget the things that shaped us in those long days of adolescence and early adulthood? Do we know where the secret confessions lie huddled like popcorn beneath folding seats on floors waxed till they shine and stink? Oh cinemas of your teenage years, the strenuous existentialism of walking with the collar of your coat turned up. Or the slick rolling of joints, and the cavalier abandon with which you attempted to carry off simple acts, as though nothing, but nothing, was a challenge to your quiet cool. Of not appearing too needy so as not to put girls off (everyone knows that) so the neediness becomes the source of other afflictions and is bad for the skin. Saturday afternoons in Portobello Road, in the sun, wondering through the cracked prism of a broken window at the absolute certainty of only one thing: that if you attempt to get up from the pavement, where the universe is remote enough to be manageable, then the fervid cocktail of drugs and alcohol will prompt complete and terminal meltdown, and you will spend the rest of the day walking like a kidnapped alien through their grimy streets with the sun casting peachy light on the facades of Victorian houses. Carol, 19, from Leytonstone, will take you to her bed but will not have sex with you, not yet, not until her girlfriend agrees to sleep with you also, in which case everything will be fine and we can travel as a threesome.

24

It is all too simple, too obvious or else too complicated. So you both make it to the kitchen where you drink gin and watch a spider working its thread above the stripped pine table. You nod your head and shrug off an encroaching hallucination. In that case, you say slowly, the words forming into little puffs that evaporate before your eyes milliseconds after speaking them, you won't mind if I eat alone. You reach for the spider, scoop it into your mouth, wash it down with gin.

These hieroglyphs are embossed into my flesh, you see: embedded markings, scars. They constitute a galaxy of wounds, sounds, incisions. They provide no answers because no questions are implicit in the hieroglyphs. The hieroglyphs are the consequence of a life spent digging the metallic earth, navigating a city of cranes and broken windows and abandoned railcars and prams left in puddles. There is a steady dripping from above, the earth is receiving its moisture back, is impregnating itself, and the wet city floats upon a wet sky, and the letters and numbers flail and fall about the place like isolate screams. The warehouse has six hundred windows, every one of them smashed. This thoroughness of destruction fascinates me. How completely someone has gone about his job of work: an exercise in mindfulness. Wrenched from a dark burrow in the fields, I wander through the warehouse, sort the hieroglyphs into order, call them my stories, my creations. I nurse them into thriving, sharp-featured beasts, feed them sheep offal and snake blood.

HOUSE

The estate agent was nearly an hour late. The agency pamphlet had informed me that it was a well-appointed Victorian detached house, in a pleasant suburb. I certainly could not afford it, but wanted to look around, and when it came onto the market I did not hesitate. I had driven past the house so many times, had felt its persistent call. Ivy on the red brick walls, an untidy, sprawling garden, sloping gradually to the south, rosebushes straggling over the edges of an expanse of lawn. I could imagine Bethan, my wife, tending the garden, and the happy cries of our children, playing on the grass. I tried the front door, and it opened. I walked inside. The estate agent had not mentioned the smell of freshly excavated soil in the cellar, the rope hanging from the rafters in the loft, the stench of gas in the kitchen, the empty bottle of barbiturates studiously placed next to the half-finished litre of vodka on the soft velvet of the living-room sofa. These were not clues; they were accusations, or even invitations towards the drawing of a conclusion, a dance of sorts, in which the steps had been traced in advance. I could hear a blackbird sing. I walked outside and watched a tree, a copper birch, as the lowering sun flecked its leaves in unreal light. I closed the door and stepped onto the gravel pathway towards my car. That night I did not return home.

Forget about writing then, he said, wringing out his sodden raincoat, squeezing the rest of his life into a grey bucket, filling a horse-syringe and fixing the sediment into his mainline. It's good to recycle, he went on, high as a kite by now, even the bits that haven't happened yet can be recycled, if you catch them in time. The past is easy; it comes on with the first rush. The future is less coherent, sure, but you can usually patch it together from what you know of the past. The only advice I would give you is to stay well clear of the present. I listened to this rubbish while trying to set a coal fire in the grate. Eventually it caught. Where would I be without firelighters? He picks up the bucket and empties it down the sink, then flops onto the sofa, the cat vacating its perch with a startled chirrup. He must have answered the door like that, wearing pyjamas under the raincoat, and spent ten minutes talking in the rain with the person he refers to as 'The Alleged Postman'. What kind of a man is that, to speak in such a way of some- one he hardly knows? What kind of a husband stands talking, in his raincoat and pyjamas, arms folded against the cold, there on the steps that lead from the front door down to road level, for all the street to see, his hair plastered to the temples and forehead by the wet, and a soppy tuft stuck up at right angles to his crown, in the manner of Tintin, the famous boy detective. It's easy, he said, to speak to the postman, in the rain. Easier than writing a novel. Easier than shooting up the past. He fishes in his pocket and retrieves two letters. I didn't want these, he says, and the man who brought them, the alleged postman, wouldn't take them back. He sits forward in his chair, looks at me. I see that he is quite deranged and decide once again that I will leave him at the earliest opportunity. He doesn't even open the letters. He throws them on the fire and after half a minute grey carbon flakes dance drunkenly up the chimney.

Looking over the city rooftops on these winter days when the sun never rises far above the horizon and then piss-weak, dispensing light grudgingly. Here the rules are queer in the extreme – and evidently so devised as to require breaking. A landscape; weather; rules. At least one of these categories is man-made. The landscape nudges memory, informs that you have been in this place before, and that it is currently inhabited. You seek to fashion yourself elsewhere, but the exhaust fumes strangle you and the fear of solitude forces you back in upon yourself. You decide not to budge. Many people have not moved, you reason. Stay put. Weather is a harder variable. Where there is none, the earth slants away into memory, preserving only a disputed sunlit childhood read about in books. Weather is sometimes tumultuous, furious and red, urging you to sleep with strangers. These are good days not to venture out, unless you feel strong enough to cope with other people's sadness. Which leaves rules. Rules carry more little rules inside their oblong heads. They carry razor-blades up their sleeves. A song floats on the evening air, laden with cherry blossom. The rules tear the song to shreds, swallow it down, lick their chops.

I needed to prepare for my journey. The mountain crossing would be hard, they told me. Snowdrifts and blizzards would frustrate my progress. Frostbite was a hazard against which there was little protection. Ravenous wolves would hunt me down and eat me. Carrion birds would pick at my remains and in the thaw the villagers would find a chalk skeleton splayed against a green hillside, the wind gasping through my ribcage. Others held to a less gloomy prognosis. I would find the partisans, they would take me in, hide me in their caves, offer me their rabbit stew, their harsh liquor. When I finally set out, Mother was tearful. I explained to her that I must go; that if the soldiers came I would be killed outright, and the village would be burned for giving me shelter. She said: There is no greater sadness than leaving those you love with no hope of ever seeing them again. I could say nothing. I picked up my gun and left in the still and freezing dawn.

There is a lunatic near here who fills large bottles with fresh water, takes them on a supermarket trolley to the nearest city bridge, and pours the contents methodically into the river. It is possible there are many lunatics by the river, but this one in particular has caught my notice. I am reminded of the scriptural enquiry: what fool poureth water into the sea? – true, this is not the sea, but it is only one mile downstream to the estuary and this stretch of river is tidal, or it was before they built the barrage. I have spoken to the man in question. He says that he is purifying the river. What, with tap water? No, he tells me, though he will not say where his bottled water comes from. Nothing is satisfactory about this. If the man, whom I call a lunatic, is sane, then he should tell me where the water comes from. If my insistence on his telling me the truth about the origins of his water seems pedantic to you, bear in mind that he might be poisoning the river, and the fishes, although he claims his purpose is to protect the wildlife. So one day I follow him. He collects water in his bottles from a little further down the river, adds a lot of salt, returns to the bridge, and pours it back. He is putting salt in the river. Restoring the nutrient balance of the aquatic ecosystem. He says the river is an open wound. He is a lunatic. Salt, he thinks, will heal the world. I know better.

How old he seemed in the dusk – how he smarted and burned inside and smiled and rolled his cigarette, reading the international news, committed now to a patching up of lives, the construction of bridges, a resolve to still the cries of orphans. In the past few years, vague anxieties had pressed upon him like the attentions of a nervous dog worrying his ankles. He had been in the Balkans and knew the counting of bodies, but still was not prepared for this. He saw the bloated corpses riding on the waters of the flooded river; he counted the cost of lives in hundreds and in thousands. He was glutted with the distress of other people. But more: he was witness to the disintegration of others' memories, puzzled by collective amnesia as much as actual genocide. His idea of God was re-awakened, ironically, by an earthly oppression he could no longer serve, or even acknowledge. There was a wilderness inside him that was more terrifying than anything he had encountered in his years as war correspondent, evangelist, murderer, thief of souls; he needed to contain that wilderness, to channel it into his thin fingers, let it scorch everything he touched. At the same time, he saw himself as a perfectly respectable horseman riding out one fine May morning across the fields of Connemara.

Miranda has the list in her jeans' pocket. She screws her hand inside, pulls out the list, smoothes it flat. There are items of fat-free food, of course, and a number of cleaning agents: detergent, bleach, scourer. She likes to keep her new flat spotless. She takes a trolley and steers it around the supermarket, tossing in the articles she requires in a way that indicates a cavalier disdain for such mundane consumerist activity. The supermarket is not her preferred domain. She holds her head high and flicks hair from her face when a man she likes the look of catches her eye. She considers herself distinct from the other people; the harassed solo women with their screaming brats or the fleecy families that always consist of mother, father, daughter, son. The dads help out. They are house-trained. They would not have lasted ten minutes in the battle of Stalingrad. As for old people, they are invisible to her: they do not exist. She wants a spotless flat and the admiration of men she sleeps with once and will not see again.

INSURANCE

Nobody told us that the annual expedition to the volcano would be cancelled this year. Many tourists had arrived to witness the spectacle of the procession as it left the village, though none would be permitted to accompany it up the mountain. Normally, the villagers, dressed only in loincloths and bodypaint, ascend the precipitous path in order to expiate the god who dwells inside the volcano. This they do with pride, and a degree of nervousness, since no one knows which of them will be turned upon and cast into the smoky pit known locally by the same name as the god who inhabits the volcano. It is said that there is no malice among these people, and it is also said that whoever is thrown into the volcano actually *falls*. He or she is never *pushed*, though they might be said to have *lost their footing*. However, this year, due to the activities of a gringo insurance company, the ancient ceremony has been abandoned. With the advent of tourism, and the resultant increase in local income, villagers have been encouraged to take out life assurance policies. Unfortunately, none of them can afford the enormous premiums demanded of them by the insurers, should they wish to take part in the ceremony that has for so many centuries set their community apart, and brought them the protection of the smoking god.

Nothing is as dismal as these days when the night never recedes far enough and the sun is obscured by layer upon layer of sempiternal grey. We who live in such places become accustomed to it but it is well known that we crave sunlight and warmth. And like plants kept in dark and unlit rooms, we do not know how to behave when the world changes and there is a freak outbreak of summer. Immediately the men stride the streets half-naked, showing off their horribly burned backs and shoulders. They have a tee shirt flapping from the back pocket of jeans, they swig from cans of beer, shout vulgar greetings to one another, drive their cars with windows down and music blaring, music that they inflict on the world as a badge of brash identity. The women, or girls, throw aside all caution, don miniscule skirts and sashay down the sidewalks with their biological imperative and urgent mating calls. The men grunt and ogle, swig their beer; the women dally and pout, showing leg and acting tough, but making rapid squeaky sounds in a bat-like call that is only detectable to certain strains of male hormone. It is another cycle, another cause for misery at the unending predictability of the genus. But on the dismal days of winter, what we'd give to replicate these scenes of summer; here by the riverside, where the ashen remains of lost sunsets wash past, the muddy water scaring us with its stain of blood-red longing.

Whatever they had been told was lies: there was no kind of deal awaiting them, no siren call. The armistice was signed but the war had been lost years before and nobody had told them. Indigo night interrupted by orange explosions on the horizon, great sweeping clouds of dust making everything invisible for hours on end, the spotlights bearing down on them the length of the assault line. *We will never know defeat*, they repeated; the words of their leader an idiot's mantra in their throats. They spent the whole day waiting for news: when should they expect the enemy? In the evening, a small group sat by the linden tree and passed a bottle around. The dusk obliterated memory. One of the men dreamed of France, a country he had never been to. People's lives there are almost perfect. Something small and forgotten in his soul told him France was a better place in which to die; that there, eternity has brushed its sleeve against the land.

Outside, there was purple weather, turning black. Like a bruise, thought Alice; a huge bruise spreading on the world's skin. She was most relaxed when she was travelling, but to nowhere in particular. Right now she was in the compartment of an evening train. She looked out of the window at castles and vineyards. This was the country she knew best. She took off her shoes and rested her feet on the seat opposite and half-closed her eyes so that the landscape took on another aspect, viewed through the veil of her lashes. She liked what this distorted vision produced; a blur of images, with a surrounding halo of violet or indigo. She was happy for thirty seconds. Then she remembered that although still young, she was already defined by the men that she had known. This was not the way she would have preferred things. She had boarded a train, the first train, and would not get off until she arrived at some distant place whose name she had not heard before. She didn't want anything, except to be travelling, on a train, to nowhere in particular, in the dusk, and by half-closing her eyes she was closer to a world that no one else could see.

'If you go to that place, you will find that water is your element. If you stay away, you will spend your life in ignorance.' Alice was not expecting this. She had gone to the Tourist Information Centre in order to garner information about bus times to the mineral springs of Kalabushi, but not this; first the psychic categorisation, now this probing for some kind of response. Alice stared at the woman who had spoken to her. She was dressed like a flight attendant, or air hostess (a term that evokes a more naïve and glamorous age of travel) with blue jacket, regulation white shirt, tacky silk scarf, and a badge on her lapel, designating her as Miranda. Make-up on her face, crimson lipstick, a professional mask. She was still smiling, this Miranda, head tilted slightly, staring at Alice a little more insistently than the role of clerk in a Tourist Information Centre required. She was waiting for Alice to say something. Alice felt the sweat prickling the back of her neck, under her armpits. She opened her mouth as if to speak, but before the words could form, Miranda had begun to throw out roots, stubbly at first, like the growths on potatoes that have been lying around too long, then thick tubers sprouting rapidly from her face, her arms, her breasts. Her smile flickered, a red sickle in the centre of her face as she spoke again, even as more shoots emerged from her cheeks, sending out tentacles questing and shimmering across the surface of the counter towards Alice. 'You see, I should know. I should know.'

39

Music cast the day open: salsa music, not what she expected. She had found this *pension* close to the station, after arriving in the city late the night before, gone to lie down on the bed, and next thing she knew it was three a.m. and she was getting cold, so climbed between the sheets, fully clothed. Now there was noise and sunlight on the streets and she felt a curiosity to explore the town. She showered in warm water and dressed. By the time she left the *pension* it was nearly midday. She passed a blind lottery ticket-seller, a youth on roller skates, an African man selling CDs (it was he whose music had wakened her), an old lady on crutches who had stopped on the sidewalk to stare at the park across the road, a dog with three legs, a fruit-vendor with the face of a young Sophia Loren, a traffic cop blowing his whistle between glances at the fruit-siren, many starlings in a tree beside a fountain, scrawny cats watching the starlings from a distance, a man in a suit drinking from a brown paper bag, a dirty café window, a row of black bags stacked beside a wheelie bin, a dog pissing against the rear wheel of a parked car, a broken television set, a spilled pizza carton – and she said to herself all this goes on, all this is connected, every single thing here is connected to every other little thing, and it goes on and on and I am not a part of it, I am not a part of it.

Ah, he is a wolf, a wolf, explained Gabriela to Alice. He has a wolf's mind and a wolf's teeth, and the long leathery tongue of a wolf, and a wolf's yellow eyes and when he rests his head on your thigh you are lost to him and the desires that inhabit his wolfish brain. Alice catapults to a realisation: that she is Morgan Le Fay and knows how things will unfold, whereas Gabriela is Guinevere, a victim to inertia and in thrall to any passing infatuation, capable of being seduced by any idea, any landscape, any wolf in any guise. In fact, Gabriela is jealous of Alice and wishes she could embrace a wolf with as joyful an abandon as Alice; Alice who doesn't care whether he is a wolf or not, who doesn't respond beyond the sense of pleasure that he arouses in her, who doesn't care for animal categories, and doesn't hang the pelts of creatures on her wall.

She wanders miraculously sane through the old port, looking for a safe place to sleep. *Best to hang out in a gang, if you're a girl.* Alice despises gangs. She would rather risk being alone, although it scares her. She sings a song, *a knife, a fork, a bottle and a cork,* yes she sings that, and she carries a knife, a bottle and a blanket. She walks quickly, eyes focused ahead. She needs to focus because stopping is not an option. She finds an abandoned warehouse, a place she has slept before. She climbs dangerous stairways to a room with broken windows. She peers out onto the quay. Cranes hang like tall sentries over the ships. Everything is corroded by sea-water and neglect and smells of rust and diesel. She settles in the furthest corner of the room, takes a candle stub from her pocket and lights it. She folds herself in her blanket and props herself against the wall. She sucks strong coarse wine from the bottle. The taste makes her want to gag, but the warmth is in her blood now. She takes the letter from her pocket, flattens it on her knee, and begins to read for the third time that day. *My darling Alice, By the time you read this I will be shooting up rainwater. I hope you suffer, as I have suffered on account of you...* She smiles and holds the corner of the letter over the candle flame.

Alice remembers standing next to a stolen Mercedes on a mountain road in Spain. She was with Luc, a thief and trafficker of marijuana. They were waiting for nightfall before crossing into France along a smuggler track through the Pyrenees. She was smoking the merchandise and staring over the hills that fell away to the sea. Her life had changed considerably. She ate in quality restaurants and dressed in silks. She no longer worked the *vendange* or hung out with the winos in *Plaza de la Trinidad*. The bonnet of the big car was still warm and she lay back on it. Luc emerged from the car, and placed his hand between her legs. She closed her eyes. When night seeped into the valley, they prepared to leave. Alice sat up on the bonnet and saw a wild boar, a sow, trotting down the track towards them, followed by two young. She was delighted, signalled Luc to be still. The large boar stopped at twenty paces from the car, sniffed the air, then turned and stared at Alice. The two young boar stopped in synchrony, transfixed. Then, with a snort and a squeal and a scraping of hooves on the dust road, the three set off at a gallop through the gorse. Alice marvelled at the strength and purpose in the sow's movement as she charged along the hillside, white tusks brushing the low grass. Alice slid off the bonnet and into the car. Watching the animals run had made her want more of everything.

'There are not many singers left in the world', said Alice, peeling a mushroom. She was right. Singers had been disappearing gradually since the autumn. Those inclined to sing haphazardly over tea, or while working in the fields, were escorted away by uniformed figures and were never seen again. There was no official interdiction, no banning order; only an oblique awareness that it was no longer acceptable to voice sounds in musical cadences or to produce a snatch of melody. The famous singers went first; opera stars and country crooners; rock idols and folkies and the gospel crowd. Choirboys, exuberant minstrels, street performers and voice therapists followed. Shower-hummers and bath-warblers were tracked down and driven away in unmarked vans, towels slipping from waists as they tried to gather an armful of songs for the journey. Even whistling window-cleaners were not exempt from the early morning walk to the warehouse wall. Alice turned from her chopping, smiled, and hummed a line from *The Sound of Music*: 'Me, a name, I call myself…' There was a hammering at the door.

THE STRANGE BIRD

Alone in her cave Alice thinks about Gabriela, and how they met. It was at the zoo. Gabriela had been working in the reptile house; Alice shovelled elephant shit. Then Gabriela was moved to the aviary, while Alice continued with the elephants. One day a small bird escaped from Gabriela's care, in fact it escaped from her hands, which opened as if by their own volition and the bird was free. It landed next to a gargantuan pile of excrement and began to peck away. Alice looked up from sweeping straw and saw Gabriela, who was peering down into the elephant enclosure, trying to locate her bird. 'My bird flew in here,' she called out to Alice, who shrugged. 'What kind of a bird was it?' she asked. 'Oh I don't know. It was a sweet thing. Blue. Or turquoise.' 'Do you mean *that?*' – Alice pointed at the bird, whose head was bobbing, beak darting in and out of the pile of dung – 'If so, it is surely purple.' And the bird did, at that moment, in that light, seem purple to Gabriela. 'Yes. That's him.' She walked over and scooped up the bird in one movement. Alice blinked. 'It's not so much purple,' she said, 'as mauve. Look.' It was true. The bird had changed colour. Gabriela started away from the elephant enclosure, then turned, and blew Alice a kiss, her lips pursed in a perfect O blowing over the ruffled feathers of the strange, multicoloured bird.

ARRIVAL

The aeroplane arrived on time and the passengers alighted, crossed to the customs building in the dark, and waited for the carousel to deliver their luggage. It was a Saturday evening in November and the airport was quiet. I sat at the edge of the hall on a plastic seat and when the conveyor belt started up, moved to pick up my luggage, a single holdall containing bread and vegetables. It joined my laptop computer on the cart and I left the hall and went to the car hire booth. The woman there checked my driver's licence and gave me the keys to a silver car. I drove for two hours, into the wilds, and came to the house, parked outside and unloaded my luggage. The key slid into the lock. The house smelled of must. I laid a fire, cut vegetables for soup, then added nutmeg, sea pebbles, mercury, a phial of petrified air, a sprinkling of memory, lizard's tongue, wren's eyes. I poured myself a drink and sat by the fire as the soup bubbled on the stove. I stared a long time into the fire; I think the wood was olive. An enormous moon began to edge across the window. There was a knock at the door and I heard someone come upstairs. I moved towards Alice and unbuttoned her overcoat. Underneath she was naked and smelled of earth and lemons. Her mouth covered mine and her secret, the one she could not tell me, slipped down my throat. My body was suffused with heat. Outside the wind was working hard, would not let up, would not let up.

46

Dusk was a word that Alice loved: saying it, she was in her element. She uttered the sound slowly, releasing the D from her palate with the tip of her tongue, like a small kiss that fluttered across the sandstone vowel, and into the Slavic cluster of the S and K. She felt she was a creature of the in-between, the liminal, and this word showed her how to shadow the day like a violet cloud, helped her dress it in sorrowful expectation; a thief preparing for the night's adventure. She was neither day nor night, neither black nor white, neither one thing, nor yet quite the other. Or rather, she was precisely other, even to herself, and her own language was always foreign to her. She climbed the red stairs slowly, looking through the tall window at the sea, tasting the salt on her lips. An unrepentant jubilation stabbed her eyes and she could tell herself: *dusk*, oh yes, I am the dusk.

I don't know where to begin. Words fall about me like leaves. Tomorrow is a call on a distant reed, tremulous and dour. The rain will come, I will construct a shelter: the winds will bring it down. I will begin again. Here there are wild animals such as you have never seen, not in books, not in life. They gather round my fire, at a distance. I do not know if their intention is to harm me. I call out to them, fling them bones, the occasional hunk of meat. They wait, careful not to break an invisible line between themselves and the fire. With dawn they drift away. I need to return to the city, to warmth and civilization, but am not certain that the world still contains such things, and in many ways feel more at home in the company of wild beasts. I have begun to dream of crowded streets and, in my dream, know that if I look long enough, I will see my own face in the window of an underground train. The train will pull away from the platform, into the blackness, and when I awaken I will be wearing a face I do not recognise as mine. Then I will know where to begin, again.

LOSS

The difficulties of holding out against the onslaught of irreconcilable loss: how did we manage to carve out such a lack in our lives? This slippery verge, where I miss my footing, and slide towards a stagnant stinking pond, this is where my scribbled notes and hieroglyphs fall from my hand and scatter, float among the weeds and sludge. This is the place where, picking up the scraps of sodden paper, they lose all sense, or else become undecipherable. Where all the accumulated fascination of the written and the spoken word dissolve into a kind of mumbled liturgy, a pidgin composed from tongues with no obvious point of connection. A place where the semblance of communication drifts away into a no man's land reminiscent of those terrible photos of Flanders where decomposing human bodies lay strewn among the broken mules and muddied skeletons of artillery, rifle butts, ownerless helmets. This is what my grandfather lived through. It's in my blood. Somehow I carry this foretaste of oblivion in my memory.

THE PAST, AGAIN

The square beneath the plane tree seems smaller now. You have not been back for many years, and when you walk around the Turkish quarter, down the narrow street, no more than an alley, where you used to live, you feel the onset of an almost unbearable nostalgia. From the church of Agios Gerasimos the priest's insistent recitation mops the morning from the sky, the old PA a crackling soundtrack to a cloudless day. You know all this as though it were an ineffable reality. A woman sweeps her porchway across the square. Her back is turned to you, so you cannot see her face. But half a lifetime away you see Aphrodite, the fat hooker with hennaed hair, who leans from an upstairs window, yawning, and a group of cats who watch one another, tails flicking, eyes blinking in the sun. It seems the town is shadowless as midday approaches, and yet along the confines of the streets behind the old harbour you walk in shadow. You learned long ago that people who move stealthily act as though they always were in shadow. You walk with such care that you become invisible.

SPY

There was a knock at the door. I got up and answered. A man stood on the porch, wearing a grey trilby. I asked what he wanted. He said he was a spy and wanted to monitor my activities. I said if he was a spy he would not tell me he was a spy. He said such an attitude was simplistic, that it was a case of calling my bluff. I conceded that what he said may be so, but listen, I said, Mister Spy, I have nothing to reveal, nothing to conceal, and am of no interest to The State; I have no politics and no opinions on anything whatever. He said that in itself was of interest, if true. I said listen, I have things to do, I am a busy man. What things? he said, you forget, I am a spy, I need to know. He gestured at the trilby, meaning, I suppose, that it represented something I would never grasp or fathom. I have things to write, I said, typing on an imaginary keyboard, as if he were an imbecile, then added, foolishly volunteering information: *though I have nothing much to say.* So then, you admit it, said the spy, with a note of triumph. If it weren't for me, coming to your house like this, you'd have nothing to say *at all.*

Miranda dreams of a perfectly quiet place, on a perfectly still shore. That is where she wants to be. Absorbing the sun, letting it flood over her skin. But she is here: she covers herself with crèmes and unguents, sits on the terrace of her high-rise apartment. Below, the city sweats and farts its way through a bad afternoon. Clouds of exhaust and the ghostly smell of burning metal climb like wraiths past her twenty-ninth storey. She lights a long cigarette and inhales. Perspiring, she shifts in her deck-chair, loosens her bra, and, on a whim, drops the article from the balcony. She watches it fall, a satin, featherweight piece of aerial flotsam: the delicate strap, the upturned, twisting cups. It seems suspended for an instant, caught in a draught or a thermal or some odd confluence of air-streams, then falls away, smaller and smaller, until its existence becomes a matter of perspective or opinion. Inspired, and with a slight tremor, she steps out of her knickers – not a thong, but a bland and diminutive slip – her fingers springing open in a star as she releases them. They too descend with the whirling abandon of a wounded bird, and though she cannot see, they land at the feet of a street evangelist plagued by erotic fantasies, who has only this minute paused in his declamations of imminent apocalypse to stare at the other article of underwear which, seconds earlier, alighted on his outstretched arm.

From my window I watch a train as it leaves the brightly-lit station, just across the river. Rain falls heavily, splintering the glare of street-lamps. Elgar, whose music I do not care for, attempts a seduction. I admire the visual articulation of a particular row of books in the corner of this book-crammed room. A rubber plant bursts up between the banister and a box of files. The cello glides uncanny in the flame of a candle, cantering now, along a receding tide, astute to the melancholy of the boy I was, catch me catch me, bury me in the solitude of dusk and I will waken one week later badder and wilder than before. A click on the sound-deck reminds me that the concerto has come to an end. Cars slosh through the street below. I open the skylight a little higher and cool night air invades my room. Another train pulls out, hauling drunks to Merthyr after a day on the lash, this one's on me boys, and the rain falls on the railtrack and the road and the houses and the river as I put on my mask and prepare for the first guest of the night.

Every stolen object tries in some way or other to return to its place of origin. Everything you touch retains the imprint of your fingers' memory. Every dusty surface testifies to the absence of human intervention. Every cycle of disbelieving victims makes things easier for the man of regular activities. Every prospective mother vexes at the overdue baby's tardiness. But my neighbour prefers sideways movements to the vertical axis. She prefers tea to coffee. She would rather an afternoon in a hammock than a vigorous mountain walk. She prefers cats to dogs, rice to pasta, seafood to meat (but red wine to white). Inside her apartment small coloured birds line the walls in cages. She has a fear of dreaming about large empty houses where she is unable to find objects of importance to her. She is happy to live alone but occasionally enjoys the company of strangers, or near-strangers, like myself. For example, she sometimes knocks on the wall that separates our two flats to signal that she is about to take an aperitif, surely an anachronistic choice of activity for a person still only in her thirties. She drinks a dry, chilled sherry; never gin and tonic. Very occasionally she will invite me to stay for dinner, but never longer. She is an indifferent cook.

I ate cold stew and wondered how long it would be
before the night sea crossing. They had been pre-
paring small fishing launches and cruisers, trawlers
and cargo ships, every manner of vessel, but still the
departure was delayed by inclement weather. I lay
concealed behind a gorse bush on the heights above
the harbour, peering down through Russian binocu-
lars. I was not certain who I was spying for. The en-
emy had attempted to recruit me and I had acceded
to their request in order to prevent them killing me.
But I had no love for the enemy. My own tribe was a
disgrace, commandeering vegetable plots and chick-
ens, putting psychotropics in the drinking water,
confiscating all the mannequins from the major de-
partment stores and lining them, in army uniform,
along the clifftops. As if anyone would be fooled by
that! There was a third allegiance I was considering,
the side which had supplied me with these fine bin-
oculars and a warm leather jacket that made me feel
like a god. It was this that tilted the balance, I think.
That evening, after my day's vigil in the gorse-bush,
I visited the local pub. Young women clung to me
(or to my jacket) as if I were a screen idol. I pleasured
one of them in a shed behind the tavern car-park.
This is the life, I thought, slinging my binoculars
around my neck and setting off through the night.

There in the woods: snow, carrion birds. I follow foot-prints. In a copse overhung by dripping branches stands a stranger, warming his hands before a fire that he has built from scraps of wood and buried pinecones. It takes a while, he says, to start a fire with damp materials. You need to keep it going, he says, you need to feed a fire. He pulls a bottle from the deep pocket of his coat and takes a slug. There is an order to the way that things are done, he says, especially in a woods. He stands on one leg and removes, first one boot, then the other, tossing them onto the flames. He splashes brandy on the fire and the boots begin to roast. Next come his socks, trousers, under-pants. For a while he stands barefoot in the snow, naked from the waist down. I cannot help noticing that his penis has shrivelled up into his scrotum. He drinks some more and passes the bottle to me. I decline. The order of removal, the man says, reflects the clarity of one's thought. My thoughts are not clear at all. Not at all. He removes his coat, and folds it carefully, dousing it in brandy, and laying it on the fire. There is much smoke, then flame. His shirt follows. Now he is completely naked. I look at him. Aren't you cold? I ask. He smiles a thin smile and takes a drink: I am never cold. He raises the bottle and pours the spirit over his hair, his face, his chest, his legs, and walks into the fire. Stop, I blurt: this is all wrong. But the man pays no attention to me. Before he burns, his face peels away in the heat, floating to the ground in a single thin film, the edges curling. I pick it up. The man has sunk to his knees and is on fire. As I leave the woods I drop his face in the snow. I do not want to walk home and have someone ask me what's in my pocket and have to pull out another man's face. When I turn around, the carrion birds are all about it, pecking, making their rough sounds.

UNCLEAN

Absolutely nothing or nobody can help you now. You are on your own. Outside a gale blows. There is a beggar lying on the porch but you cannot let him in. He will bring pestilence, disease and chaos. His name, you have been informed, is unpronounceable except to those who speak the dialect of a part of the country you have never visited. A beggar then, whose name you cannot speak, whose needs can never be satisfied, and whose gift is turmoil. But you need to pass him if you are to leave the house. So you assume a disguise, open the front door, step onto the pavement. The beggar appears to be asleep. You ring your bell, clutching your hood tight around your face. 'Unclean,' you say, voice quaking: 'unclean.' The beggar whose name you cannot say lifts his head. His eyes are bloodshot. He smiles up at you and from deep inside his coat produces a black snake. He holds it above his face for an instant, then drops it into his upturned mouth. The tail enters last, thrashing from side to side. He belches, wipes his lips and lies down again, turning his back to you. The depth of his breathing tells you he has fallen straight back to sleep.

RIVER JAZZ

The sound of a far-off saxophone brought him back to consciousness. All day long he had lain between woods and water, sleeping. By evening, gnats buzzed across the surface of the river and trout began to jump. It was late August, and there was an edge of electrical activity to the air that presaged a storm. Cows were lying down in the field across the river. But this music, this weird tattooing on the evening's skin, disturbed him. There was nobody in sight. He threaded a fly and stepping barefoot into the water, cast across the river to a spot beneath the overhanging bushes on the far bank. The line jerked and he tugged upward on the rod. The rod bent into an arc, the pressure forcing him to step back towards the bank, one leg still in the water. As he struggled for his footing on the smooth pebbles, the rod flicked free, dropping into the water. From the far side, a tall woman with a shaven head and scaly skin emerged from the water, blowing into an alto sax, followed by a full jazz orchestra of fish people. They crossed towards him and climbed from the river in doleful procession, not missing a note. They vanished into the trees.

Alice said that time was running out. Dark poison clouds hung above the city, and the few who ventured out wore masks or held handkerchiefs to their faces. I went and spoke to her. How can you be so sure? I asked. She gestured out the window. Are you blind? she said. Things looked pretty bad out there: crashed vehicles, some overturned like stranded beetles; the smoking pyres of charred animals; the river flowing slow and thick, like treacle beneath our high-rise office window. It was months since I'd heard a bird sing. It was months since clean water ran from the taps. So what shall we do? I asked her. She was impassive, hands on hips, staring at a point beyond my head. Some will turn it into an excuse for a great debauch, she replied, while others will scurry to their Gods. Most will simply try to find a place to hide. And you? I asked, trembling. I am going to a place beyond salvation, where there are no rules and no questions asked. Let me go with you, I pleaded. No, she said, if I wish to take a lover, I will find one there, among the men who live like beasts, think dark, and know no charity. That way, there are fewer complications. I saw that she was adamant; and if I were her, with all she knew about catastrophe and pestilence, I would have made the same decision.

THESEUS' SECRET SHAME

I wanted to write a hieroglyph on your body, to write the scent of you, the curve of your neck as you slept, the improbable heat that rose from you, the arm bent back across your face: Ariadne in repose. So where to begin? I sculpted myself into the hollows of your flesh, tasted you, began to write a poem on your thigh. The world caved in. I awoke in the maddening dawn, at Naxos, encrusted with salt, circumscribed by your absence. Turning, I discovered you had written hieroglyphs all over me instead, before you left.

The dogs were out, hunting through the ruins of
the amber city in packs. Occasional tarpaulins and
barricades of hastily-assembled brick and timber pro-
vided refuge for a few surviving citizens. The air was
so acrid and stale that it burned my throat. I sat in
the rubble with a bottle of looted vodka and Filos,
my old sheepdog: I didn't care. But the dog had more
sense, and led us to the ruins of a library, where we
climbed the stairs and found a corner by the only
stained-glass window that had not been blown in.
That afternoon there was bad music in the air. Sur-
vivors were falling about and the dust was impreg-
nable. I saw a pack of dogs converge on one man,
hopelessly drunk. He slipped and fell and the dogs
were onto him. They ate him alive. Filos whined at
my side. He had a strong sense of a dog's place in the
universe: it was in his breed. I fed him some smoked
sausage and settled back with a book. Any book. I
had the whole library and no social obligations to
attend to. I could take my time. I pulled a book at
random from the shelf nearest and read for a while
about the adventures of a young man who is cap-
tured by a tribe of primitive people, cannibals, who
make him their king. I looked out of the window
again. The dogs were still around the body of the
fallen man. The pack leader was sitting apart, lick-
ing the blood off his coat. A puppy was chewing at
the man's ankle. A strange dog, with a tan coat and a

loping stride, approached the body. The pack leader scrambled to his feet and snarled at the newcomer. He was not one of them. The strange dog moved away slowly, looking over his shoulder. The rest of the pack was watching him. He began to run, vanishing into the smoke and rubble and detritus of the city. As he disappeared, Filos nuzzled at my shoulder. I gave him another piece of sausage.

He enters a village, walks over to the well. He drinks and sits in the shadow of a tree. Realising that he has visited this village in a dream, he sets out to find a house. In the house he knows he will find what he is seeking, has always sought. The streets are narrow and no one is about. The sun burns the back of his neck. Soon he discovers that these narrow alleys are a labyrinth. Each passageway resembles the one he has just left. The upper stories of the whitewashed walls slant streetward, occluding sunlight. He walks in silence and there is no one of whom to ask directions. Ahead, he sees an arch that leads into a courtyard and another whitewashed house; this one has pots of red flowers hanging from hooks beside the door. All the rooms are empty, except the last. It is perfectly clean. A white room and a bed, draped with fine muslin netting. He is tired, he undresses and leaves his clothes scattered on the floor. He pulls aside the netting and sees the woman he knew would be there, lying on the white sheets. As he lies down next to her he feels a tremendous sadness. His body trembles with the grief of an entire lifetime. He wants to speak but knows that the woman will not respond. He closes his eyes.

SWAMP

The forest was sinking. The creatures that lived there were half-submerged in swamp water. At night, the smaller animals struggled to climb a few remaining stumps of trees or rotting logs that protruded above the stinking surface. I was attempting to wade across this bog, from east to west. It was a very long journey and everyone warned me against it. But there was no way around. Several days into the journey, I began to experience a liquefaction of the soul and an aquefying of the senses. Next, a watery element began to replace the more familiar shape of my lower limbs. The legs attained a status something like wet clay, but becoming more porous by the hour. Gradually the process rose through my body, and as I became more of a fleeting thing, the transparency of my skin revealed rivulets of swamp water where there had once been veins of blood, and a jellification of my organs was clearly in progress. As my body hair fell out and the surface of my body resembled a shiny smooth slime, I began to move more easily in the water, aquiline, head uplifted, surging forward without causing a ripple, silent, like the stinking green virtuous things around me, heading west, dissolving into water.

They invented a machine that characterized distinct modes of sleep, another tool for categorising the artefacts of the human mind and hastening it towards the desert of broken objects. Your own sleep was marked by well-defined parameters of rapid eye movement and involuntary jerking of the limbs, like a dog who dreams that it is running through an open meadow of wind-blown grass and poppies. The machine also posed demands for information, such as: *Who were you before?* A question poorly-framed but typically astute. It reminded me of staying at the Villa Ranchetti in 1977, and of the boy who asked: *What happens to the little Francesco once I have grown into a big person?* To which the answer might run: if you are lucky, he stays with you, alongside, or inside the person you will become. I failed to mention that in most cases, the child is murdered in his sleep. I failed to imagine that they would one day have a machine which assisted in that solemn infanticide, and which would afterwards provide a breakdown of imagery considered appropriate for dreaming, and those other things that were deemed unnecessary or decadent. Dreams of being a child fell into this category, along with elephants, dancing foxes, all marsupials, fresh mint from the herb garden, formations of water-birds crossing the wide sky, the smell of the sea at daybreak, silent waves, a full moon.

THE ROAD NOT TAKEN

There was a fork in the track. I chose one of them, assuming the other to be the road not taken. After a few minutes I returned to the fork, chose the other one. It looked much the same as the first, though I knew that by taking it I was messing with fate. Within an hour or so, the road originally taken had become the road not taken, and I had to invent some kind of alternative destination for it. I decided that all outcomes are, to a large extent, the result of will. It was then that I realised I had lost my shadow.

PIANO BAR

The piano swerves upward, slaying notes in sweep-
ing strides, blasting startled epiphanies of cold air
between clods of earth that spatter the walls with the
explosions that precede each ascending scale. There
is a Russian song lost in the damage being done; it
has been absorbed into the sponge of your listening
ear. The music churns around you like an icy sea.
Afterwards the pianist speaks of a letterbox
overspilling with mail and a house that has been shut
up for a decade, the door so stiff, it needed to be
lifted off its hinges, shutters encrusted with the
memory of salt. Seeing Gabriela across the bar after
all these years, a smoky lustful intimacy being blown
in my direction, her half-averted eyes, the slightest
suggestion that she might smile; but not yet.

Call up, 1914. A line of conscripts are handed their uniforms, tin cup and plate, a list of duties. It is a cold evening. Two years later, outside the smoking ruins of a village in France, those who remain alive huddle close for warmth. The sound of sporadic shellfire. It is autumn. They pass around cigarettes and drink muddy tea. My grandfather rubs grit from his eyes. He lights a Woodbine, spits, looks up at the sky. To the east, something is starting. It looks like a fireworks display. Grandfather, whom a lifetime later we call *Taid,* feels the cold water seeping through the sole of his broken boot. The rain comes down, gentle. Around them there is nothing but desolation, mud and water. *Taid* is a corporal. He is talking with his men in Welsh. Three hundred yards away, another corporal, with an Austrian accent, is talking to his men in German. One of them will become a mining engineer in Machynlleth; the other will try his hand at painting.

There was a high-wire artist in her life, a man she could only ever imagine way above the crowds, looking straight ahead. His single-mindedness was a quality she admired beyond all others in a man: to keep his whole attention fixed upon a point, and work towards it slowly. In this respect she felt she quite resembled him. He became her focus, the object of her gaze. She wondered at his skill and balance. Watching how he took his time, but with such grace, convinced her that these talents would be transferable to the art of making love. She dreamed about him and determined that he would grace her life, perhaps forever. She instigated a determined courtship, over lengthy dinners in darkened restaurants, and later, in the comfort of her silk and satin furnished luxury apartment. It was only when she finally possessed him that she recognised her own obsession's inevitable outcome: that her great desire was to see him fall, to watch that spectral figure, high above the buildings, topple, hesitate, suspended in a zero gravity, and then the long descent through gasps and exhalations, the same white noises of ecstatic plunging that she made, alone, at night.

DOG BREATH

There was a hammering at the door. I was expecting a delivery of some kind but had forgotten precisely what. Two men stood outside. The one who did the talking told me they had brought a sofa, and I remembered the arrangement we had made; although, as I recalled it, it had been for that afternoon, not this morning. They took a long time filling out a document, then brought the sofa inside. My dog began to bark from the next room. The first of the delivery men, who was above average height and had curly brown hair, began to bark also. His barking was neither louder not quieter (though less convincing) than that of my dog, who, after a brief pause, took up his barking again with some vigour. When the two workmen had left the sofa where I wanted it in the hall, the taller one, the one with curly hair, turned toward me and barked again. His face was too close to mine. His breath smelled of dog.

He liked the women of Madrid: there was an insouciant quality to their laughter, a preference for surprising bedroom games and a guileless predictability to their acts of revenge. He was charmed too by the extreme sociability of the species, their willingness to experiment, and a tendency to being unfazed by his peculiar and unpredictable shifts of identity. So, for example, one day he could claim to be an Englishman working on secret government business (inviting comparison with Commander James Bond, the renowned British agent) and the next an Azerbaijani poet forced into exile; the third a world-weary doctor with *médecins sans frontières*. It was not lost on him that the admirable traits he attributed to madrileñas might have been evidence of the travails of his imagination, rather than of any objective reality, but he was happy to sustain this fiction as it made him feel perceptive in his knowledge of women in the wider world: 'ah,' he could say to one of his male companions, 'but *you* do not understand the women of Madrid!'

He had woken from the anaesthetic dreaming of the sea. He was parched and hungry and in a stubborn effort to retain the maritime flavour of his dream, craved a tuna sandwich. However *Nil by Mouth* was posted at his bed-head and he endured both this craving and his thirst with the martial, dogged humour that had marked his illness over several months. His wife sat by his side, a warm and subtle presence, holding his hand, and he enjoyed the visit of the surgeon, asking when the monstrous battery of farts that issued from his strangely detached body would ease up. He experienced a vaguely surprising need to pat his dog's head, to stroke the floppy ears, a desire that he abstractedly considered not to be quite appropriate, given the prohibition of dogs from hospitals, most especially from Intensive Care. Within an hour or two of waking he had drifted back to sleep and found himself upon a makeshift raft, the endless ocean swelling placidly around him, sharing tuna sandwiches with his dog, a variety of spaniel. He scoured the horizon for any hint of land. Night was falling. He could hear nothing, and the gravity of silence made him turn: a massive liner was bearing down on them, a million lights ablaze along the bows, lights that flickered into knowledge of something vast, unstoppable.

I do not know quite how long ago this all began. Struggles with the preterite. I might have to go right along the finger-tips of memory, to somewhere hidden by a matrix of words learned in a phrase-book and in a language whose use and currency I have now abandoned. But we were there and the pictures bear testament to this fact: your sandalled foot brushed by sand, my fine straw hat, the yellow buoys that flecked the bay and rocked on the tide, and the surf, which crashed in sun-specked fury on the shore; the clutch of upper-crust tourists striding into the restaurant with the confidence granted by one's natural ascendancy; the elegant couple by the plane-tree who, we conjectured, had arranged this meeting through some chic dating agency, so measured and beguiling, as the mutual recognition of attraction so transparently progressed. And when we stood on the castle walls, the sea and the plains laid out all around us and the distant mountains shadowing tiny white villages, it was then I remembered what I had been told: it's hard to alter the course of our destinies once they're underway, if we don't yet know that they're our destinies. Let's weave a magic bag instead, to store your glass beads, along with a note that conjugates the verb 'to be'.

TRANSLATION

All your stories are about yourself, she said, even when they seem to be about other people. I was not going to deny this, nor give her the pleasure of being right. So I quoted Proust, who said that writers don't invent books; they find them within themselves and translate them. This seemed to do the trick, and she fell silent. I dipped my fingers into a bowl of scented water and started on the rice. An aftertaste of clay and leaves and metal took me by surprise. What is in this rice? I asked her. Mushroom stock? Shotgun cartridge? Earthworm? No, she said, peering at me through the candlelight, the stories that you haven't written yet are in the rice. You must be tasting them.

BALLAD OF THE SAD GIRAFFE CAFÉ

In the Sad Giraffe Café one bides one's time. Pebbles of conversation that patter like droplets of embodied sound, the swish of the waiters' extravagant robes. Windows, vast and tinted with the colours of your thought, give out onto a landscape that is somehow unfamiliar despite your having spent so many years within these walls. They say the secret of the Sad Giraffe lies in the way, each time you enter, it provides a new texture to the experience of your being there, so that you never know if, truly, you are witnessing the products of your own imagination or whether all that occurs within the Café happens for the first time, once and once only. It is also said, by men of a literal cast of mind, that those who stay too long in the Sad Giraffe Café grow very long necks, but we, the guardians of the place, know better: the Café exists only for as long as and to the extent that we, its creators and tenants, re-tell and repeat its story, unspooling and re-threading the narrative day after day, night after night, replenishing ourselves as well as it, the Café, with the illusion of its existence.

RICHARD GWYN grew up in Crickhowell, South Wales. He studied social anthropology at the LSE and worked in factories and as a milkman, before leaving London to spend ten years in aimless travel, settling for periods in Greece and Spain. He returned to the UK in the 1990s and took a PhD in Linguistics at Cardiff University, where he now directs the MA in Creative Writing. He is the author of five collections of poetry and two novels, *The Colour of a Dog Running Away* and *Deep Hanging Out*. In addition he has written many articles and essays and reviews new fiction for *The Independent*. He has translated poetry from Spanish and Catalan, and his own poetry and fiction have appeared in several languages. His website can be found at *www.richardgwyn.com*

Recent titles in Arc Publications'
POETRY FROM THE UK / IRELAND,
include: